Introduction

1 Timothy In-Depth Bible Study
Fight the good fight

Thank you so much for reading this book. I understand that there are other study guides available, so I really do appreciate you taking the time to read mine. As for this book, I give all the glory to God. Without Him, this wouldn't be possible.

You may notice that some passages were skipped, this is because I did not feel it on my heart to touch base on them. Therefore, there will be some gaps.

Throughout this study, when I refer to the enemy, I always use a lowercase letter, even if it's the first word in the sentence. I know that it may sound odd, considering we are taught not to do this, but this was intentional. So often we give the enemy power in our lives. Through anxiety, fear, depression, or whatever else it is that you are going through. I wanted to show you that he has no hold on a child of God. So when you see these "grammar issues", know that they were done on purpose. Use them as a reminder that satan has no hold on you. In the name of Jesus, you don't belong to him. You are God's, and God's alone.

1 Timothy 1:4

When Paul urged Timothy to stay in Ephesus, he wanted him to charge some people to teach no other doctrine. To stop giving thought to lies, untrue stories, and endless genealogies. At this point in the bible, Jesus had already died and rose again, so everything had changed. The inheritance that was initially only belonging to the Jews, was now no longer only belonging to the Jews. Whether you came from the line of David, or from the line of a Gentile, if you believed in the death and resurrection of Jesus Christ, and you believed that Jesus was Lord, you were a son of Abraham, regardless of genealogy. This same fact holds true today. God doesn't care more about the Jews than He does everyone else. If you look at a Jew that is a believer, and one from another descent that is a believer, it makes no difference in God's eyes. He doesn't show favoritism. We are all equally loved in His eyes.

For God does not show favoritism.

Romans 2:11

Maybe you think that someone who study's the bible more, is favored by God. That couldn't be farther from the truth. Maybe you think that someone who does more good things, is loved more by God. That couldn't be farther from the truth. Maybe you think that your past defines who you are, and maybe you think that you have to earn God's love. Again, this couldn't be farther from the truth.

No, in all these things we are more than conquerors through him who loved us. For I am convinced that neither death nor life, neither angels nor demons, neither the present nor the future, nor any powers, neither height nor depth, nor anything else in all creation, will be able to separate us from the love of God that is in Christ Jesus our Lord.

Romans 8:37-39

Nothing can separate you from God's love, and nothing can make God love you more than He already does. He already loves you with a perfect love. If you are someone trying to gain God's love, I want to assure you, He already loves you perfectly. He loves you so much, that He took the form of a man, to die a painful death, just so that He could one day be with you. What greater love is this? Than to lay down His life for His friends. Jesus took the pain of all of your sins, and He bore your debt. He suffered, for love. So if you ever think that you have to gain that kind of love, look at that cross. You didn't earn His love, He already gave it to you before you came into existence. He already knew you before you were born. And to go a step further, He already knew His plans for you.

"Before I formed you in the womb I knew you,
before you were born I set you apart;
I appointed you as a prophet to the nations."

Jeremiah 1:5

This scripture clearly shows that before anyone is born, before anyone comes into existence, God knows them. This is the powerful God we serve.

So in this particular verse we are reading, Paul is telling Timothy to not give any thought to things such as genealogies and fables. They do nothing but cause arguments with one another. Instead, God wants us to stop the foolish arguments, to stop comparing, and to lift one another up. To talk about things that matter, things that increase learning, things that are of faith, things that help others gain understanding.

Remember, if you think that the Jews are God's chosen people, remember that when Jesus died, everything changed. A Jew that is a believer, and you who are a believer, are all EQUALLY God's chosen people. No one is above the other.

But you are a chosen people, a royal priesthood, a holy nation, God's special possession, that you may declare the praises of him who called you out of darkness into his wonderful light.

1 Peter 2:9

1 Timothy 1:5-7

To love from a pure heart. I would look at this as loving regardless of what you get in return, loving those who are hard to love, and loving all shapes, sizes, races, and ethnicity's. Loving regardless of your past, your status, your age, or anything else.

Love is patient, love is kind. It does not envy, it does not boast, it is not proud. It does not dishonor others, it is not self-seeking, it is not easily angered, it keeps no record of wrongs. Love does not delight in evil but rejoices with the truth. It always protects, always trusts, always hopes, always perseveres.

1 Corinthians 13:4-7

Here Paul is saying to love from a pure heart. Also from a good conscience. If you do something for someone thinking that they will give you something in return, that's not a pure conscience. A pure conscience is doing something for someone, and expecting nothing back in return. He also says to do this with sincere faith. Some people talk with words, but not with truth. They desire to be a teacher of the law, but they know nothing about the law. They state things as true, but they may go by hearsay or made up words, and are nothing but a mere rumor.

This leads me to tell you to be careful with what you hear, and who you listen to. There are many wolves among the sheep, and they are disguised as your friend. Some seem to be highly knowledgeable, and they may be, but they subtly plant false truth with the real truth, so that you don't even know that what you are being fed, is a lie. Think of it as a Mom who gives a child something good to eat, but then plants vegetables inside, so you can't see or taste them. This is the same as wanting to be fed the good stuff, the word, but then being fed things that don't taste good and aren't nourishing for your soul. You don't notice it because it's mixed in so subtly with the good stuff, that you don't even know that it's there. Now obviously vegetables are good for you, but I hope you get the point that I am trying to make.

Behold, I send you out as sheep in the midst of wolves. Therefore be wise as serpents and harmless as doves.

Matthew 10:16

There are false prophets everywhere. They are claiming to be a teacher of the law, and claiming that they are sent by God, but be careful. Pray and ask God to reveal to you anything or anyone that comes in your life or near it, that you will know who is of God, from God, and for God. I pray for those of you who are believers with me, to have a strong discernment in the truth. To know when something is false, and to have the wisdom to know when you should and should not be listening to someone. If anything at all is telling you that something doesn't sound right, check it. Compare it to the word of

God. Don't just shun your feelings away. If you are feeling anything at all, consider it enough to look into it. If you are wrong, so be it, but if you are right, you saved yourself from receiving false doctrine. Either way, whether you are wrong or right, I truly believe that God would honor the fact that you were trying to make sure that you remained in His truth.

1 Timothy 1:8-10

The law was made not made for the righteous.

For sin shall not have dominion over you, for you are not under law but under grace.

Romans 6:14

But now, by dying to what once bound us, we have been released from the law so that we serve in the new way of the Spirit, and not in the old way of the written code.

Romans 7:6

This does not mean that you should go on sinning because you are not under law, but grace.

What shall we say, then? Shall we go on sinning so that grace may increase? By no means! We are those who have died to sin; how can we live in it any longer?

Romans 6:1-2

If you are a true follower of Christ, you no longer want to sin. You are a new man, a new creation. You no longer want to follow the ways of the world, but of Christ. When you follow Jesus, you want to be like Jesus, you want to act like Jesus, walk like Jesus, take up your cross and follow Jesus. You may no longer be under the law, but you still want to follow the law. Why? Because you love Jesus. When you love someone, you want to make them happy. When you love someone, you spend time with them, you give up things that you want to do, for things that they want to do, and you sacrifice your needs and wants, for their needs and wants. When you truly love Jesus, these things hold true as well.

Now there are some who are asleep. Some who became sleepers and who no longer follow Jesus the way that they used to. My hope is that the sleepers eyes may be open, and that they may remember who they are in Christ. Not for my sake, but theirs. This is why it is extremely important to stay in the word of God. satan is crafty and he will subtly try and get you away from God little by little. This is why you must remain alert and sober. As the enemy prowls around like a roaring lion, seeking who he may devour.

Be alert and of sober mind. Your enemy the devil prowls around like a roaring lion looking for someone to devour. Resist him, standing firm in the faith, because you know that the family of believers throughout the world is undergoing the same kind of sufferings.

1 Peter 5:7-9

Don't let your circumstances make you stray from the truth. Don't give the devil a foothold. Know that you are not alone in your sufferings, as all believers around the world, myself included, are also enduring hardships and sufferings along side you. We do it for the glory of God. We do it because we love Him. It's not an easy path, this is why the bible says it is narrow. It's hard and difficult, but the reward is great. Jesus is enough of a reward to have, by following in His footsteps. Don't let anyone deter you or change your path. Stand firm with me and know that you are never alone.

And the God of all grace, who called you to his eternal glory in Christ, after you have suffered a little while, will himself restore you and make you strong, firm and steadfast. To him be the power for ever and ever. Amen.

1 Peter 5:10-11

1 Timothy 1:11

You were entrusted with the gospel. What are you doing with it?

Please read Matthew 25:14-30.

1 Timothy 1:12-16

Paul, who has written this letter to his son Timothy, is telling him that he (Paul) was ignorant. That Paul was the chief of sinners. He did wrong, but yet he obtained God's great mercy, because he did all of these wrongdoings in ignorance. The definition of ignorance is lacking knowledge, information, or awareness about a particular thing. He acted out in unbelief. But, Paul received mercy from God. He then tells us that God gave him grace in overflow. He uses the word exceedingly. So Jesus exceedingly and abundantly gave him grace. One that he didn't deserve. But is this not why Christ came into the world? To save sinners? He didn't come for the well, but He came for the sick. I find it beautiful that the next part in 1 Timothy 1:16, Paul tells us that Jesus showed him mercy for a reason. The reason is to show how patient Jesus is with us. To show us that this is the pattern of Jesus. That He is patient with the unbelieving, the ignorant, and the sinners. He is patient because as we see in 2 Timothy 2:19, "*The Lord knows those who are His*". He knows who will eventually come to Him and believe in Him, and He knows those who are His. It's like me saying to God, why do you put up with them? They are blaspheming you and they are persecuting those who believe in you. God, why are you so patient with them? And it's like Jesus right here is responding to this. I am patient with them because they are mine. They belong to me and I look forward to the day that they believe in me, and moreover, I look forward to the day that I can spend eternity with them. It's like He is responding to the question of why are you putting up with them. And His response is, because I love them. I find this so beautiful.

I also want to point out that Paul is giving God the glory and honor for the ministry that he has. Not once did he say, I have this ministry because I worked for it, I gave it to myself, and no one helped me but me. He says just the opposite. He thanks Jesus, and he thanks Jesus for giving him the authority to even be able to have his ministry. Considering that he is far from perfect, as we all are, yet Jesus still allows us to be a part of His world. I am sure that Paul never had a dream of being in the ministry, as he always persecuted the ones who followed Christ. This is a perfect example of God wanting something opposite of what you wanted for your life. I heard someone say something once. I don't remember the exact words, but it was along the lines of this.

I don't want God to be centered around my life, I want to be centered around His.

It feels like it's saying this. I don't want God to be centered around my wants, my needs, and my dreams. I want to be centered around His. I want what He wants. His thoughts and ways are higher, and so, He knows way better than I do. If I center Him around my life, He is coming into my wants and my needs, but if I surrender and allow myself to be a part of what He wants for me, then He will lead me to a way better path than I could ever choose on my own. Let me give you an example. I used to want to be a singer. At times, I still do. But, I didn't make that what I had to do. I laid it down and died to myself. I gave it to God. I told Him that if He gives it back, I would gladly take it back, but if He didn't, I would gladly lay it down. At this moment in my life, I feel Him wanting me to write. This was not something that I had on my list of dreams, yet, God wanted me to do it. Sometimes I try to go back to wanting to sing again, but God shows me that it's not what He has planned for me at this moment. And you have to remember that just because something is a no for now, doesn't mean that it's always a no. It could be just a no right now, or a no forever, but either way, I am willing to let go of the things that He doesn't want for me, even if it means going in a different direction than I had planned.

A man's heart plans his way,
But the LORD directs his steps.

Proverbs 16:9

My point is, when you go into God's world, which this is just a metaphor for going to Him in full surrender of your needs and wants, you are laying your hopes and dreams at His feet, and you are leaving them there. You are saying God, I fully surrender these to you, and whatever you have for me I'll do, regardless if it's on my hopes and dreams list or not, because my hopes and dreams are you. I care more about what you want, because that's how much I love you. Is it hard? Yes, at times it is. Sometimes you feel like things are moving so slow and you just want to take things into your own hands. But let me remind you, God's plan is better than you could ever dream of or imagine. And while at times you may try to take back those dreams, just remember to ask yourself this. Do I love God, more than I love these dreams? And the answer, should always be yes.

<u>1 Timothy 1:17</u>

No one is wiser than God. He is the wisest of the wise. Remember, He founded the earth by wisdom.

*The L*ORD *by wisdom founded the earth;*
By understanding He established the heavens

Proverbs 3:19

Please also read Proverbs 8:22-31.

Proverbs 3:7 also tells us, "*Do not be wise in your own eyes*".

God alone is wise. This doesn't mean that we can not have wisdom, or attain her, because the bible clearly states that we can. For example, James 1:5 says this.

If any of you lacks wisdom, let him ask of God, who gives to all liberally and without reproach, and it will be given to him.

You would be quick to think that all you have to do is ask. But when you look at the context of this verse, you will see that there is something that you are required to do on your part.

But let him ask in faith, with no doubting, for he who doubts is like a wave of the sea driven and tossed by the wind.

James 1:6

This is another conversation all together. If you want to know more, please read my study guide on James.

What I am getting at is this. God is eternal, immortal, invisible, and wise, among many other things. No one is above or before Him. He is in His own area, because no one and nothing compares to Him. Sometimes we forget that God is more than someone who we just pray to. He is all knowing, all powerful, all places, at all times, etc. Our God is not someone who just sits there listening to your prayers, He is doing things. He is working on things, in your life, and in others lives. God knows exactly what He is doing. You can trust Him. Don't forget to remember the God you serve. He is a good God, and if you are in the middle of a battle, He's with you through every step of it. He is working on things even as you are even reading this. He is always working. Everything is going to be OK. Just trust Him.

1 Timothy 1:18-20

In this life, we face conflict. It's a given. You can't escape it or hide away until it's gone, because it will eventually find you. Whether it's money issues, work issues, marriage issues, mental health issues, health issues in general, etc, there is always something. We are at war with the enemy. In Ephesians, we see clearly where this war comes from.

For we do not wrestle against flesh and blood, but against principalities, against powers, against the rulers of the darkness of this age, against spiritual hosts of wickedness in the heavenly places.

Ephesians 6:12

Don't be so quick to say that your spouse is giving you a hard time, or your job, or a co-worker, etc. We must remember as believers, there is a curtain. The one behind the curtain comes to kill, steal, and destroy. We are at war, and so often we think that the war is with each other, but we couldn't be more wrong. We all need to come together and realize that the same enemy messing with you, is the same enemy messing with me. Or at least he tries to. Sometimes he succeeds, but that's a struggle we all face. I wrote a book called Breaking chains: The diary of a woman who overcame anxiety. It has my journey with anxiety along with some lessons that I felt God had put on my heart to share. One of the parts was me talking about satan as an equivalent to a fly. He buzzes around you and you swat him, and around you, and again, you swat him. The fly buzzes in your ear whispering lies, and at first you don't believe them, but as time goes on, it's sometimes hard to keep those noises out. That's why we need the word. It swats that fly and his lies. The only way to successfully kill satans lies, is to find the truth that defends what he is saying is false. For example, if he is telling you that you are a mistake and shouldn't have been born, find truth. The truth is that God chose you. John 15:16 says "*You did not choose Me, but I chose you*". There are a lot of scriptures that tell you who you are in Christ. You were chosen, set apart, you have a purpose, you are righteous because of what Jesus did at the cross, God has a plan for you, your past is forgiven, God watches over you, and God loves you, just to name a few. If you ever find yourself struggling with a lie of the enemy, find truth.

I believe that Paul is trying to tell Timothy here, that even though he has to go through warfare, as do we all, that he should approach it in a way that makes it good warfare. Let me explain. We all go through things in life, trials, hardships, etc. How we face those trials and hardships, matter. They should matter to you, but they matter most of all, to God. God wants us to handle our circumstances in a way that pleases Him, and in a way that shows that we trust Him. Bad warfare would be me kicking and screaming at the drop of a dime. It's the why me, and the why can't I just, and the if only, that are considered bad warfare. We are meant to keep our faith in all situations. Is it easy? Of course not! But the more you have faith in all circumstances, the more your faith grows. The more in turn, you please God. Because as we know, without faith, it is impossible to please God.

But without faith it is impossible to please Him, for he who comes to God must believe that He is, and that He is a rewarder of those who diligently seek Him.

Hebrews 11:6

Another way to have good warfare, is keeping your conscience clean. If someone throws insults at you, and you respond with insults back, that's not good warfare. That's adding fire to fire, and evil for evil. Do what's right in God's eyes. Don't worry about what they are doing, worry about what you are doing, and how you are responding. Ask yourself, does this please God, would this let my light shine, did Jesus act this way towards others? Jesus didn't return insults for insults. He overcame this world, so can you. In 1 Peter 2:23, it clearly tells us how Jesus acted towards these people.

who, when He was reviled, did not revile in return; when He suffered, He did not threaten, but committed Himself to Him who judges righteously

Jesus entrusted Himself to His Father. The same Father that we should entrust ourselves to. You don't have to seek revenge or look for a way to get someone back. We are supposed to love. Yes, even our enemies. Matthew 5:42-45 even goes further as to say to not only love your enemies, but to bless those who curse you, and pray for those who spitefully use you and persecute you.

Give to him who asks you, and from him who wants to borrow from you do not turn away.

"You have heard that it was said, 'You shall love your neighbor and hate your enemy.' But I say to you, love your enemies, bless those who curse you, do good to those who hate you, and pray for those who spitefully use you and persecute you, that you may be sons of your Father in heaven; for He makes His sun rise on the evil and on the good, and sends rain on the just and on the unjust.

Matthew 5:42-45

I leave you with this. Overcome evil with good.

Do not be overcome by evil, but overcome evil with good.

Romans 12:21

Don't engage in warfare the same way as your enemy does, as this is not the will of God. We are not meant to be like the world, but to stand out from the world. To come out from among them, and be separate.

Also, concerning your faith, don't let it be shipwrecked, as some have already done. A shipwreck suffers loss. Loss of boat, loss of items, and even loss of a person. If you lose your faith, you can't please God. Faith is at the core of our very being. How can you follow God, when you have no faith in Him to lead you? I get it, warfare is hard, I can attest to that. I've been through a lot myself. Some days, are harder than others, but it's not about how many times you fall, it's about what you do with the fall. It's how you get back up. It's how you react during the fall. Do you still praise God and tell Him that you love Him, do you tell Him that you need His help, and do you rely on Him? Everything should always lead back to God. Even if you are so numb that you just can't move, still, tell God that you love Him and you need Him. I have been strengthened more times than I can count, by a loving God who always finds me when I just want to give up. One night I may go to bed crying, and I can't move because I am so numb, and the next day, I wake up and I have joy. That's not a coincidence. That's God. That's Him being faithful to me, even when I just feel as if things will never change. That's the God we serve. One who is faithful, even when we are not. One who loves us, even when we don't respond correctly to situations. He is a good God, never forget that.

If we are faithless,
He remains faithful;
He cannot deny Himself.

2 Timothy 2:13

1 Timothy 2:1-4

If you see here, Paul uses the word, for all men. He is stating that this is what we should be doing for others. Praying earnestly for others, giving thanks for others, etc. This could mean praying for someone else's situation to get better, for their circumstances to change, or for them to come to know Jesus Christ as their Lord and Savior. It also states to pray for kings and all who are in authority. This means that we should be praying for our nation, for the president, and for all who are in authority. For those of you who focus on politics and don't like the president, the mayor, or even your boss, pray for them. Pray that God is with them in their decision making, and that the choices they make honor God. You may not agree with someone, but that doesn't mean that you can't pay for them. We are to pray for all people. Whether they are believers or not.

"You have heard that it was said, 'An eye for an eye and a tooth for a tooth.' But I tell you not to resist an evil person. But whoever slaps you on your right cheek, turn the other to him also. If anyone wants to sue you and take away your tunic, let him have your cloak also. And whoever compels you to go one mile, go with him two. Give to him who asks you, and from him who wants to borrow from you do not turn away.

"You have heard that it was said, 'You shall love your neighbor and hate your enemy.' But I say to you, love your enemies, bless those who curse you, do good to those who hate you, and pray for those who spitefully use you and persecute you, that you may be sons of your Father in heaven; for He makes His sun rise on the evil and on the good, and sends rain on the just and on the unjust.

Matthew 5:38-45

Do good to those who hate you and PRAY for those who spitefully use you and persecute you. We are meant to pray for one another and lift one another up, regardless of how they are treating you, or have treated you. Why? Because this is what we are called to do, and because this is what Jesus did. We see this clearly in 1 Peter 2:21-24.

I leave you with this. Pray for everyone. Pray for them and leave your focus on God. Reverence Him, love Him, and remain in awe of Him. Don't get distracted by the things of this world. This is a tactic of the enemy, to get your eyes off of what truly matters, God. Don't let him succeed. Stand firm with me.

We also see that praying for others, is good and acceptable to God our Savior. God desires for all to come to Him and be saved. He wants all people to know the truth, and that the truth may set them free. This is why

God will give the same person chance after chance after chance. He doesn't give up on us. He is a good God and He wants us to love Him, but He won't force us. And I for one, am grateful that I was given the choice. Some people may wonder why God doesn't just force us to love Him and follow Him. Ask yourself this question. If you have a child, would you feel better if you "made" them love you, or if they loved you just because you are a good parent? If I forced my child to love me, I would know that they didn't truly love me. I would know that the love was only being given to me because they had to, not because they wanted to. It's a different feeling when you know someone genuinely loves you, rather than because they have to. Have to love, isn't real love, and because I was graciously given the choice, I can now say honestly, that I truly do love God. Not because I am being forced to, but because I truly do love Him. I love Him because of so many reasons, but it all boils down to this. He is a good God. And if you think about it, we love Him, because He first loved us.

We love Him because He first loved us.

1 John 4:19

He took the time to show me His love. He took the time to protect me, comfort me, give me provision, help me in my deepest valleys, cared about me when I was scared, carried me when I couldn't move, took on my debt before I was even born, and so much more.

We love Him, because He first loved us.

24

1 Timothy 2:1-7

There is only one mediator between God and men. Jesus can not be substituted for anyone else, ever! You can't know the Father, unless you know the Son. If you do not know the Son, then you do not know the Father either, it's that simple. You can't put it any other way, and nothing else makes sense. Jesus died so that the wall of separation was torn, so if you remove Jesus from the equation, that wall is still there.

And Jesus cried out again with a loud voice, and yielded up His spirit.
Then, behold, the veil of the temple was torn in two from top to bottom; and the earth quaked, and the rocks were split, and the graves were opened; and many bodies of the saints who had fallen asleep were raised; and coming out of the graves after His resurrection, they went into the holy city and appeared to many.

Matthew 27:50-53

This was all because of Jesus. There is no one other man who has the power to forgive sins.

But that you may know that the Son of Man has power on earth to forgive sins

Luke 5:24

Nor is there salvation in any other, for there is no other name under heaven given among men by which we must be saved.

Acts 4:12

*I am the LORD, that is My name;
And My glory I will not give to another,
Nor My praise to carved images.*

Isaiah 42:8

Jesus gave His life as a ransom for ours. All believers are appointed to spread this good news of the gospel. To go into all nations, telling them about our Lord and Savior Jesus Christ.

And He said to them, "Go into all the world and preach the gospel to every creature. He who believes and is baptized will be saved; but he who does not believe will be condemned.

Mark 16:15-16

This commission is not for a select few. It's for all believers. This means that you don't have to be a preacher to preach, a teacher to teach, or anything of that matter. This means that all of us have a responsibility to tell others about Jesus Christ. We are called to teach in faith, and in truth. We know and believe Jesus to be our Lord and Savior, and we know that He died and rose again. We share the love of Christ, because we too believe in Him, and because we have faith in Him as well. When we share Christ, we do it through the faith that we have in Him, through His Holy Spirit who guides us into all truth. We do it, because we love Him, and because we want others to experience how amazing He is.

Let's make heaven crowded!

1 Timothy 2:8

We should be praying everywhere. Whether we are at the store, work, school, etc, we should be praying in faith, without doubting. I believe that we should be in constant contact with God throughout our day and night. We are told to abide in Him and He in us. This means to remain in Him, and Him in us. Just as a plant without roots withers away, so do we when we are not planted in the Lord, if we are not planted in His word, and if we are not remaining in Him. We need Him for our nutrients, and for our daily bread. We can not simply sustain ourselves. We are not sufficient enough to sustain ourselves. We need God for this.
As we are told in Ephesians, we are to put away all wrath.

Let all bitterness, wrath, anger, clamor, and evil speaking be put away from you, with all malice.

Ephesians 4:31

27

Wrath in the dictionary is defined as extreme anger. Anger does not produce the righteousness that God desires in us.

So then, my beloved brethren, let every man be swift to hear, slow to speak, slow to wrath; for the wrath of man does not produce the righteousness of God.

James 1:19-20

We should not be doing things in anger. When you pray, when you praise, or when you are doing anything, put your anger away from you. Cast it far away from you as it does not please God.

1 Timothy 3:1-13

A bishop has authority in the church. Someone who has any authority over another human being, should be someone who sets a good example for others. If you see a person in the church who has authority over anything, and they are coming in drunk, they curse all the time, and they are confrontational, would this set an example for others? We have to be careful who we choose for leadership in our churches, because we are setting the stage at showing others what is OK. To clarify, I am not saying that the church is meant for perfect people, no, it's just the opposite. We are to welcome everyone, even drunks and people of the world. Why? Because is this not what Jesus did? Did He not eat with tax collectors and sinners? Jesus came not to judge us, but to save us.

And if anyone hears My words and does not believe, I do not judge him; for I did not come to judge the world but to save the world.

John 12:47

We are to be helping these people, not shunning them away and talking behind their backs. If someone comes into your church, and they are acting worldly, profane, etc, don't shun them, help them. If they came there just to socialize and meet people, help them meet Jesus. We are to be God's hands and feet. We are to help everyone, regardless of race, gender, status, how they look, act, etc. Please read Matthew 25:32-46. When you stand before Jesus, will you be happy with the way that you acted towards others?

I also want to clarify that you don't need to be perfect to be a bishop, because that would mean that no one would ever be a bishop! As we know, no man was perfect, except Jesus Christ. I felt I needed to clarify these things, so they are not taken out of context. I am not saying that you need to be perfect to be a bishop, I am saying that you need to be following God, gentle with everyone, not argumentative, and not prideful. People should also not have a bad testimony about them, for example, they all say that he is a party person, and he gets so drunk every time that he falls over, etc. You need to set a good example for others, because at that point, you are moving from a member of the congregation, to someone in authority.

A deacon must be in awe of God, they must love God. Serving with a pure conscience, and not with selfish motives, self-sufficient attitudes, etc.

There is more on being a deacon here, but I think I will end the topic here with this. If you are wanting to be in any position in the church, ministry, etc, make sure that you are doing it for the right reasons. Make sure that you are abiding in God, and make sure that you have His approval to do anything. Seek His counsel, seek His guidance, and seek His peace.

1 Timothy 3:14-15

Some may forget that when we enter the church, or anywhere for that matter, there is always someone watching the things that we do. It could be the church, your work, or even your home. It could be your kids seeing how you act, your spouse seeing how you respond to arguments, your co-workers seeing how you handle that belligerent customer, or your church seeing how you care for others. We are to conduct ourselves in a manner worthy of our calling. Why? Because when others see us, they should be seeing Jesus. If your co-worker knows that you are a Christian, but you don't act like it, how would that bring them to Jesus? How would that make them want to get to know Jesus Christ? But, if stand out, and act different than everyone else, they will wonder what the reason for it is. They will wonder why you have so much hope, love, and peace, even in difficulty. They will want, and seek what you have. And you would be able to humbly tell them, that it's available to them as well. Free of cost.

But sanctify the Lord God in your hearts, and always be ready to give a defense to everyone who asks you a reason for the hope that is in you, with meekness and fear; having a good conscience, that when they defame you as evildoers, those who revile your good conduct in Christ may be ashamed.

1 Peter 3:15-16

1 Timothy 4:1-5

Some people have wondered off so to speak. They left behind one of the main ingredients of being a believer. They departed from their faith. As we know, without faith, it is impossible to please God. People are being deceived. They are straying from the truth and they have forgotten their armor. Forgotten who they are in Christ. People are believing false doctrine, and they are believing lies. For example, one says it is bad to eat meat because of this or that, but God created these foods to be received with thanksgiving by those who believe and know the truth. Every creature of God is good, and nothing is to be refused if received with thanksgiving, for it is made holy by the word of God and prayer. I want to give another example here. Some people say it is wrong to kill deer or anything for meat. I believe it is only wrong if it's done harshly, and without thanksgiving. To clarify, if you are killing an animal only to mount it's head on your wall, and dispose of the meat, then this is senseless killing. That animal died for mere amusement, instead of nourishment to your body. These are living, breathing creatures, and if you are killing for the sport of it, then I look at it differently. But, if you are killing something to eat it, and you do this with thanksgiving, then this is another story. Someone who does this with thanksgiving, and then mounts the animal, could be doing so out of thanksgiving, and not wanting to waste anything. It can have a different meaning, when done with thanksgiving in your heart. The point is, we can be deceived into certain things when we give ear and heed to deceiving spirits and false doctrines. We must be careful with what we hear, and how we hear it. Another example is people who use God's name in vain. Some have been deceived into believing that as long as you are not doing it with malicious intent, then it's OK. I see people using God's name in vain in so many places. Whether watching TV, movies, or even in real life. It baffles me how someone can think that blaspheming God is OK, as long as it's done without malicious intent. This again, is a perfect example of someone being deceived into thinking something is OK, when it clearly, is not. I could keep going with examples, but I am sure you get the point. We need to keep guard 24/7, because the enemy is prowling around, seeking who he can destroy. God gives us the wisdom, the strength, and the knowledge, to fight this. He gives us the power to trample the enemy and his many lies. The enemy is a deceiver, and he seeks you 24/7, so you need to be on guard 24/7. If you knew that someone was standing outside of your home daily, waiting for you to fall asleep so he can rob you, would you not set up a security system, would you not be on guard, would you not be prepared to fight at a moments notice? Be on guard then, and stand firm against the schemes of the devil.

1 Timothy 4:6

Brethren, if a man is overtaken in any trespass, you who are spiritual restore such a one in a spirit of gentleness, considering yourself lest you also be tempted.

Galatians 6:1

We are told to correct others. Not harshly or with anger, but gently. If they choose not to listen, then you know that you still did as God asked, regardless of the outcome. This does not mean to make a list of what someone is doing wrong and hand it to them, but what it means is, it's OK to instruct others in the way they should go. I understand it may be hard to say, and hard for them to hear, but it is necessary. Let me give an example. If I start cursing here and there, I would want my spouse to bring this to my attention. If he came up to me and yelled at me and told me how I am not being Godly, and what I am doing is wrong to cut it out, I would not perceive it well, and would most likely, get upset. But, if he came to me gently and said, I just wanted to let you know that I noticed you cursing a lot. I wanted to bring it to your attention so you knew about it. I would most likely know what he was getting at and say thanks for letting me know. I would ask God for His forgiveness, and ask God to help me correct it. If I didn't understand what he meant, then I could always say, what do you mean? The point is, you get more with honey than vinegar. If you are trying to

34

help someone correct something that they shouldn't be doing, then there is a way to go about it. Anger is not one of them. Gentleness is. Ask the Holy Spirit to guide you and help you speak with gentleness. Also ask the Holy Spirit to open their heart to the words you are about to say, and let them receive it with open arms. Sometimes they will receive it nicely, sometimes they won't. Either way, you will know that you did what God wanted you to do, and if you did it gently, you will know that you tried to do it in the best way you knew how.

Think about it this way. If you are putting a piece of furniture together, you have a set of instructions. Those instructions were not placed there to hurt you, but to help you. In the same sense, instructions are not told to make someone feel bad, it's to help them with ways on how to be more like Jesus Christ. It's to help that person build themselves up in a way that honors God. You are doing it to help them, not hurt them. You are doing it from a pure heart, not a judging one, unless you too want to be judged.

Judge not, that you be not judged. For with what judgment you judge, you will be judged; and with the measure you use, it will be measured back to you. And why do you look at the speck in your brother's eye, but do not consider the plank in your own eye? Or how can you say to your brother, 'Let me remove the speck from your eye'; and look, a plank is in your own eye? Hypocrite! First remove the plank from your own eye, and then you will see clearly to remove the speck from your brother's eye.

Matthew 7:1-5

I also want to say that if you are on the receiving end of the instruction, listen. Don't get upset, and listen. Think before you speak and get angry. It is possible that the person on the other side is only trying to help you. We can be so quick to get upset at things, because we feel as if we are being attacked. So before you respond, think. Think and ask the Holy Spirit to guide you and help you understand if you truly are doing something wrong. Don't be so quick to get offensive, and remember to listen. This includes listening to the other person, as well as listening to the Holy Spirit, who is guiding you into all truth.

1 Timothy 4:7

Reject the things that you know are untrue, and the ones you are unsure of, stand it next to the word of God. Don't let any false doctrine seep through your armor. Keep a tight seal on your mind, and reject all false doctrine. Don't even think on it. If you know it is wrong, reject it. If you allow your mind to think upon something that is false, you allow it to have time to seep into your mind, which is never a good thing.

Remember, if it is false, reject it, don't think on it. If you are unsure, check it next to the word of God, and see if it stands the test. If it's false, then again, reject it, if it's 100% true, then you can let it seep in your mind, but only if you are 100% sure of it. Be careful what you let in. One false story can lead to the next. You have to guard your mind at ALL times. Don't rest. The enemy doesn't rest, neither should you. Keep your mind guarded and protected with your armor, this includes prayer. Read the word of God, and fight satans lies with truth, just as Jesus did when He fasted for 40 days.

Then Jesus was led up by the Spirit into the wilderness to be tempted by the devil. And when He had fasted forty days and forty nights, afterward He was hungry. Now when the tempter came to Him, he said, "If You are the Son of God, command that these stones become bread."

But He answered and said, "It is written, 'Man shall not live by bread alone, but by every word that proceeds from the mouth of God.' "

Then the devil took Him up into the holy city, set Him on the pinnacle of the temple, and said to Him, "If You are the Son of God, throw Yourself down. For it is written:

'He shall give His angels charge over you,'

and,

'In their hands they shall bear you up,
Lest you dash your foot against a stone.' "

Jesus said to him, "It is written again, 'You shall not tempt the LORD your God.' "

Again, the devil took Him up on an exceedingly high mountain, and showed Him all the kingdoms of the world and their glory. And he said to Him, "All these things I will give You if You will fall down and worship me."

Then Jesus said to him, "Away with you, Satan! For it is written, 'You shall worship the LORD your God, and Him only you shall serve.' "

Then the devil left Him, and behold, angels came and ministered to Him.

Matthew 4:1-11

1 Timothy 4:8-11

If I walk on a treadmill everyday for 30 minutes, it profits me a little, but, if I exercise myself in reading the word, being more like Christ, and prayer, then it gains much more. It is useful in all things. Therefore, bodily exercise is useful in little, and Godliness is profitable in all things.

We know that we have the promise of God in this life, and in the next. In this life we work hard and suffer, but we do so willingly because we know what is our end. We know that this life is not where we end, it's only where we begin. We know that suffering will end. Yes in this life, but mostly in the next. We trust in the promise of the living God. The promise that when this life is through, heaven is waiting for us. I suppose if we did not know what was after this life, we would not be so quick to persevere. We would give up. Why? Because why would we feel the need to press on? We would be living for nothing. Our life would be meaningless because we would assume nothing when this life was over. We live, then we die. We work for nothing, press on for nothing, have hope, in nothing. I suppose you would press on for maybe a family member, a child, or a friend, but that only goes so far. Eventually, you would wonder why you are even here, why you even try anymore, as you always fall short anyways. Instead, those who believe now have this promise. This promise so graciously given to us through our Lord and Savior Jesus Christ. The promise that we will fall short, but we are still loved. The promise that our perseverance is never for nothing. It's not only helpful in this life, but it also serves as an eternal purpose. We may not know exactly how it works, but we trust in the One who does. We trust in His promises.

Therefore we do not lose heart. Even though our outward man is perishing, yet the inward man is being renewed day by day. For our light affliction, which is but for a moment, is working for us a far more exceeding and eternal weight of glory, while we do not look at the things which are seen, but at the things which are not seen. For the things which are seen are temporary, but the things which are not seen are eternal.

2 Corinthians 4:16-18

So although we can not see what is eternally waiting for us, what we do know, is Jesus is there. And where Jesus is, this is where I want to be. So we look to the things that are unseen. We look forward to the day when Jesus calls us home. We look forward, not backwards. We run our race, because we know where it leads. Into loving arms.

This is why we teach others about Jesus. This is why we share the good news. This is why we spread the gospel. Because we want others to know that we don't press on for nothing. We want others to know that there is hope in a Savior who loves us dearly. A Savior who says that we are forgiven, loved, and chosen. Regardless of past mistakes, regardless of who you are, you are loved.

People who don't know Jesus, what do they live for? What do they die for? What hope do they have in the perseverance of this life? Tell them.

1 Timothy 4:12

Let no one look down on you because of your youth. Always be an example to other believers, regardless of your age. You could be 15 and have more wisdom and knowledge than an 80 year old. Age does not always mean wisdom. If you are older, do not look down on a younger person. Whether a believer is young or old, they are still called by Christ. One member is not more important than the next, as we are all called by God, and all loved the same.

1 Timothy 4:13-14

Until Jesus comes back for us, we must stay planted in His word. We must teach, urge, and encourage others, this includes encouraging ourselves. We must pay attention to SOUND doctrine.

Do not neglect the gift that God has given to you. If you don't know exactly what that gift is, ask, and believe that you will graciously receive His answer. Don't doubt. Even if you haven't heard back, keep asking, keep asking for clarity, wisdom, and understanding. Keep knocking, keep seeking.

Don't stop asking until you hear back.

And He said to them, "Which of you shall have a friend, and go to him at midnight and say to him, 'Friend, lend me three loaves; for a friend of mine has come to me on his journey, and I have nothing to set before him'; and he will answer from within and say, 'Do not trouble me; the door is now shut, and my children are with me in bed; I cannot rise and give to you'? I say to you, though he will not rise and give to him because he is his friend, yet because of his persistence he will rise and give him as many as he needs.

"So I say to you, ask, and it will be given to you; seek, and you will find; knock, and it will be opened to you. For everyone who asks receives, and he who seeks finds, and to him who knocks it will be opened. If a son asks for bread from any father among you, will he give him a stone? Or if he asks for a fish, will he give him a serpent instead of a fish? Or if he asks for an egg, will he offer him a scorpion? If you then, being evil, know how to give good gifts to your children, how much more will your heavenly Father give the Holy Spirit to those who ask Him!"

Luke 11:5-13

Also believe. Believe that you have already received whatever it is that you are asking for. Be so full of faith in your asking, that you already believe you have it.

42

Therefore I say to you, whatever things you ask when you pray, believe that you receive them, and you will have them.

Mark 11:24

In the beginning of this book, we see that it is addressed to Timothy. This however, goes for all of us as well. Do not neglect your gift. Whatever God is calling you to, or telling you to do, do it. If you are 100% certain it's God, but you are just afraid to step out, re-evaluate your thoughts. Remind yourself that stepping out of God's will because you are too afraid to do something, is not a good reason to not do it. There is never a good reason to disobey what God is asking you to do. Instead, you need to step into what He is calling you to do, and trust Him in the process. A lot of times, that breakthrough that you have been looking for all this time, is just past that fear. A lot of times the enemy will place fear and doubt in a certain spot, because he doesn't want you to breakthrough. Instead, he wants you stuck. Stuck in your head, stuck thinking you can't do something, and stuck in general. What you need to realize, is that God will only take you so far. Meaning that He can tell you flat out what you are meant to do, but unless you take the step to do it, He won't force you. Let me clarify. Let's say that God is telling me that I need to move to another state. I 100% know that it's God. He wants me to sell my home and move. I now have a choice. I can choose to listen to God, or ignore God. This is what I mean by God will only take you so far. If God is constantly telling me what's best, and I am constantly ignoring Him, He won't force me to do the things He is asking. Why? Because He wants obedience. The obedience brings the blessing.

Behold, I set before you today a blessing and a curse: the blessing, if you obey the commandments of the LORD your God which I command you today; and the curse, if you do not obey the commandments of the LORD your God, but turn aside from the way which I command you today, to go after other gods which you have not known.

Deuteronomy 11:26-28

If you fully obey the LORD your God and carefully follow all his commands I give you today, the LORD your God will set you high above all the nations on earth. All these blessings will come on you and accompany you if you obey the LORD your God

Deuteronomy 28:1-2

1 Timothy 4:15-16

Meditate on the word, day and night. Meditate on all things of God. Whether it be your conduct, your attitude, compassion, love, sound doctrine, etc. Others should be able to see the growth that is in you. When we stay in God's word, when we stay in prayer, and when we stay grounded in God, we grow. We have no choice but to grow. To be more like Christ. When I say we have no choice, it means that when you are following Christ, and rooted and planted in His word, you just naturally start becoming more and more like Him. It's what is produced as you become more and more grounded in Him. And when you walk with God, truly walk with Him, your attitude, your conduct, and everything about you starts shifting and becoming more and more like Christ, which others see. When others see how you behave, and how you act, this will not only save you, as now you are becoming more like Christ, but it will also save those who witness your change, witness who you are becoming, and witness the change in you, one that's for the better. So it not only saves you from missteps, it not only saves you from going down the wrong path, but it also helps others from those missteps as well. This is why we should always lead by example.

1 Timothy 5:1-2

Have you ever heard the saying, respect your elders? I believe this to be true, but I also believe that you should respect all people. Older men and woman as fathers and mothers, and younger as brothers and sisters. Be respectful to all, regardless of age, and do so with a pure heart.

1 Timothy 5:3-8

If a widow is in need, we are to help them. If a widow has 10 children and 15 grandchildren, then those children and grandchildren should be the ones to act in a way that pleases God, and help them. Just as that widow took care of their child when they were younger, they should do the same, because this is good and acceptable to God.

Even unbelievers provide for their household. Even unbelievers love and care for their children and their family. We should be willing to do the same, when we have the means to do so. I say this because if I am on the streets with no home and no money, I obviously couldn't provide money, shelter, or food for that person, however, I can still provide emotional support. There is always something that you can do to help, not just financially. I believe that emotional support allows for much healing in someones life, more so than any amount of finances could bring.

On a side note, I also want to add that you should always be willing to help those who are in need. This could be pertaining to many things. It could be regarding shelter, food, or even emotional support. Let me give an example to clarify. If your child is now 50, and they lost their home, have no money for food, and have no where to go, then it falls on you to provide if you have the means to do so. Meaning that if you yourself have a home, you should open the doors with open arms, regardless of how much it will cost you for them to stay there. We all go through struggles in this life, and if you are only worried about your own life and your own struggles, what good is it? Where is the merit in that? If I say I help myself when I struggle, who would give ear to that? But, if I say that even in my struggling, I help those who struggle, than which is better? I say that it is better to help all who are in need when you can, even if you yourself are struggling. Do you think that God will be pleased with someone who only helps themselves, or those who help others?

We also need to learn that when we are on the receiving end of this, that we have to be humble enough to accept the help from others, because that help initially comes from God.

I also want to add a note about helping others. If you are helping someone, whether through money, your home, items, etc, don't hold it over them. For example, if you opened your home to your 50 year old child, don't tell them how hard it is having them there, how much it costs you for them to be there, etc. This would be equivalent to me giving you a gift, and then telling you how much I don't want you to have it, how much it cost me, how I really don't want you to take it, but I have to, etc. If you are going to give, give. Don't make the other person feel bad for taking the gift. If anything, it will make them feel terrible about themselves and their situation.

Remember, give when you can, be humble enough to take the help being offered to you, and never make someone feel bad for taking the help that you offered.

1 Timothy 5:17-20

You shall not muzzle an ox while it treads out the grain.
Deuteronomy 25:4

Do you not say, 'There are still four months and then comes the harvest'? Behold, I say to you, lift up your eyes and look at the fields, for they are already white for harvest!
John 4:35

Provide neither gold nor silver nor copper in your money belts, nor bag for your journey, nor two tunics, nor sandals, nor staffs; for a worker is worthy of his food.

Matthew 10:9-10

And remain in the same house, eating and drinking such things as they give, for the laborer is worthy of his wages.

Luke 10:7

For it is written in the law of Moses, "You shall not muzzle an ox while it treads out the grain." Is it oxen God is concerned about? Or does He say it altogether for our sakes? For our sakes, no doubt, this is written, that he who plows should plow in hope, and he who threshes in hope should be partaker of his hope.

1 Corinthians 9:9-10

A worker is worth his wages. If an elder is ruling well, then he deserves double honor, especially those who study and meditate on the word of God and it's doctrine, and preach it well and truthfully. When an ox would tread out the grain, the ox would eat it as he is treading. If someone were to do this task by hand, it would be a large task to do. Therefore, the ox is worth the wages that he is eating, because he is a good worker. A good elder who works hard and works for the Lord, is also worth his wages.

If someone makes a claim against an elder, make sure that there is also another witness. For example, if someone says that an elder is constantly coming in drunk, I am sure that there will be more than 1 person coming to you with this news. I am sure that if he is truly coming in drunk this often, someone else is sure to take notice as well.
Rebuking someone in the midst of others, makes another person fear this same rebuking. For example, if someone

comes into the church speaking false doctrine, rebuking them in front of others, makes the hearers wise to be sure to speak the truth, so that they think before they speak, and make sure that the message they are spreading, is true, lest they be rebuked too.

1 Timothy 5:21-22

Keep the instructions that God has given you, without showing favoritism to anyone.

Do not quickly give someone the position without careful thought. If you are to make someone an elder, be sure to pray about it as well. Meditate on it, pray about it, and seek God's guidance. Quick decisions are usually bad decisions. This statement could go for more than choosing an elder. Being too quick to jump into a marriage, a home purchase, a job, a financial decision, etc, is never a good way to go about things. About 7 years ago, we were looking for a home. Every home that we went to, I said we'll take it. Even homes that were falling apart! One home even had the walls water damaged by what we were told was the bathtub overflowing! My husband had to constantly say, let's think about it. Every time, when I had the time to think about it, I realized that it was far from a good choice. This happened multiple times. I was so excited that I wasn't thinking. I jumped at every home that we came across. If it wasn't for my husband's wise decision to think on it, we would have been stuck in a home that we were not happy in, or one that caused us a lot of financial issues. This is a perfect example on making a quick decision, and it's consequences. I have since learned that making quick decisions is almost never a good thing. Take your time and pray about things. Whether it's hiring someone in your church, or everyday life, include God in ALL of your decisions, and always ask for His guidance. He always knows best. His thoughts and ways are always higher than ours.

"For My thoughts are not your thoughts,
Nor are your ways My ways," says the LORD.
"For as the heavens are higher than the earth,
So are My ways higher than your ways,
And My thoughts than your thoughts.

Isaiah 55:8-9

I also want to add that if you have asked God, and are still waiting, be patient. God will answer when the time is right. Trust Him.

<u>1 Timothy 5:23</u>

No, this passage is not telling you that you should get drunk on wine. If you read the context, it clearly states that he is telling Timothy to drink a LITTLE wine, not for pleasure, but to help with his stomach. It says for your stomach's sake and your frequent infirmities. The definition of infirmities is "physical or mental weakness". By this, we can clearly see that he wanted him to drink it because of his stomach. If you were to do a little research, you would see that wine is good for your stomach. It actually helps with quite a few things in your stomach. Therefore, no, this does not mean getting drunk on wine for pleasure is a good thing. This was only said to help his stomach. This is also a perfect example of how sometimes we can so easily take things out of context in the scriptures. We have to be careful to read the context surrounding the text that we are reading, to give us better understanding. I am sure that a lot of us have made this mistake at least once before. The mistake of thinking that a scripture meant something, when it didn't. This is why it's always good to not only read the context, but to pray for clarity, wisdom, and guidance when reading the scriptures. Bible studies also help you find clarity as well, but be sure to hold it against the scriptures. If something sounds off in the writing, make sure that you pay careful attention to it, and hold it up to the scriptures, asking God for wisdom, clarity, and discernment to know if something doesn't sound right.

Some people are wolves in sheep's clothing. Meaning that they may seem to be someone who is knowledgeable, and someone to take studies from, but they are actually seeking to place false doctrine in your mind. I say this out of love, so that you take careful thought to what you hear and read, lest you unintentionally stray from the truth.

1 Timothy 5:24-25

Some people's sin is apparent. For example, someone who mistreats everyone they meet, is harsh, rude, etc. Some however, have sins that are not so apparent. Maybe it's a man who goes to church, behaves like a believer, and then goes home and becomes a person of the world, because he only wants to follow God one day a week. Some men you will see their sins in this life, and some will enter into judgment.

Likewise, some people you can see their good works, and they are clearly evident. Like a person walking an elderly woman across the street. Maybe it's someones children showing with their conduct that they follow and love the Lord. You can clearly see that good works are being done, even if you can not physically see the good works, you see what they produce. Some people, however, do good deeds all the time, yet they may think that no one sees, but God does. Just as God sees the sin hidden in one

53

man, He also sees the good deeds that are hidden in another, because nothing is truly hidden from God.

Nothing in all creation is hidden from God's sight. Everything is uncovered and laid bare before the eyes of him to whom we must give account.

Hebrews 4:13

On a side note, do not do good deeds just so men can see them. Do not let your left hand, know what your right hand is doing. We don't do good deeds to be seen or glorified by men, but instead, we do them to glorify our Father in heaven. We seek not to please man, but God.

Take heed that you do not do your charitable deeds before men, to be seen by them. Otherwise you have no reward from your Father in heaven. Therefore, when you do a charitable deed, do not sound a trumpet before you as the hypocrites do in the synagogues and in the streets, that they may have glory from men. Assuredly, I say to you, they have their reward. But when you do a charitable deed, do not let your left hand know what your right hand is doing, that your charitable deed may be in secret; and your Father who sees in secret will Himself reward you openly.

Matthew 6:1-4

1 Timothy 6:1-5

This can also be used as an example for today. If you have an unbelieving boss, parent, or anyone else for that matter, this goes the same for them as it did back then. Yes, this is talking about bondservants, meaning slaves, but I believe that the word still pertains, no matter what era we are living in, the bible can still be applied to the current day. So in this case, I would say that whatever you do, in word or conduct, do it all for the glory of God. Respect them, and show them mercy, as our Father is also merciful towards you. Do not give them a hard time, and be sure to carry the name of Jesus well. Maybe, if they see your good conduct, you may even be able to bring them to Christ!

If they are believers, still, do the same, as they are your brothers and sisters in the Lord. Show good conduct and be respectful to them, as they have received the same inheritance through Jesus, just as you did, and God dearly loves them, just as He dearly loves you.

It is good to teach these things. If anyone teaches otherwise, and goes against what the Lord asks of us, withdraw yourself from these people. People who use profane and crude words, people who teach against what Jesus has taught us, and decides to go his own way, and against the doctrine that we know to be true, he is but a proud person, knowing nothing. His mind is corrupt and void of the truth. One who is obsessed with arguments and disputes, which only come from and produce envy, strife, etc. Separate from these people. Come out from among them and be separate.

Do not be yoked together with unbelievers. For what do righteousness and wickedness have in common? Or what fellowship can light have with darkness? What harmony is there between Christ and Belial? Or what does a believer have in common with an unbeliever? What agreement is there between the temple of God and idols? For we are the temple of the living God. As God has said:

"I will live with them
and walk among them,
and I will be their God,
and they will be my people."

Therefore,

"Come out from them
and be separate,
says the Lord.
Touch no unclean thing,
and I will receive you."

2 Corinthians 6:14-17

1 Timothy 6:6

Are you content with what you have? Do you yearn for more money, a better job, a better marriage, a better home, a better life? Where does it end? Do you realize, that unless you are content with everything, you will never be happy? You will want that better job, and when you get that better job, you will eventually want more. You may say, but I only want... I tell you that it never ends. Once you want one thing, you will want another, and another, and another. You will never be happy, but always live in a state of want. I believe that the devil uses this to his advantage. If you are so focused on the things of this world, then you are less focused on what God wants in your life, and on the plans that He has for you. Let me tell you something, God has great plans for you, but unless you learn to take your focus off of the things of this world, then you may never get to see those plans while living on this earth. The path is narrow and so difficult. Few find this path because it is not easy. If anyone ever told you that being a Christian was easy, then they are not doing something right. It's hard. Following Jesus is so hard sometimes, but the reward is so much greater than the pain. Why do you think that we are told to take up our cross and follow Him? Do you think that when Jesus took up the cross, it was easy? Of course not! It was painful. His life on earth was far from easy. He was beaten, spit on, betrayed, etc. So we take up this same cross, and follow Him. We live with Him, we die with Him, even if that means a life of suffering. Why? Because we have the promise that heaven is waiting for us. And no, it's not the streets of gold that I look forward to, it's eternity with a God who loved me so much, that He died for me.

1 Timothy 6:7-8

I am reminded of a scripture in Acts.

All the believers were one in heart and mind. No one claimed that any of their possessions was their own, but they shared everything they had. With great power the apostles continued to testify to the resurrection of the Lord Jesus. And God's grace was so powerfully at work in them all that there were no needy persons among them. For from time to time those who owned land or houses sold them, brought the money from the sales and put it at the apostles' feet, and it was distributed to anyone who had need.

Acts 4:32-35

Every single thing that you own, and all of your possessions, are going to one day, be no more. That item that you won't let anyone touch, it's just sitting there collecting dust, the grass that you won't let anyone step on, because it has to be green, or that item no one can use, because you don't want the wear and tear on it,

58

gone, all of it gone. You brought nothing into the world, and you take nothing out. When I wrote the grass part just now, I was reminded of a time when I had my first baby. I took him to a garage sale, and he was tiny, still in his little car seat. There were no spots in the driveway at this garage sale, so I parked in the front on the grass, so I wasn't in the street. I got out of the car, and the man holding the garage sale screamed at me for being on his grass. It wasn't a nice, would you mind parking on the street, or waiting for a spot to open, but it was a full blown angry response. He treated me as if I was nothing. And it goes to show you, that the way you treat people, matters more than how green your grass is. I had forgotten all about this moment, until now. It's crazy how something can happen in your life, and it seems terrible at the time, but God had planned to use that incident later on, for good. This is a perfect example of how God sees ahead of us, and works all things together for good.

So ask yourself this, can you take your grass with you to heaven? Can you take that item that you won't let anyone use, with you? This is why this above scripture in Acts reminds me so much of this passage in Timothy, because all believers were one in heart and mind. They shared everything that they had, and they even sold their possessions so that no one was in need. Why don't we do this today? Why don't people share what they have, give the excess that they don't use, and love each other as if it was themselves? I don't want to be remembered for how stingy I was with my possessions, I want to be remembered for being loving, sharing all that I own, and caring for everyone. When you see Jesus face to face, I don't think He will be asking you how nice you kept your things, or how many possessions you owned. But, He will separate the sheep from the goats. He will be pleased with you for those you have helped along the way, and the people you gave to, shared with, and treated kindly. As Paul says in this letter, he was content with having food and clothing. Nothing else made any difference, because we weren't placed on this earth to see who can have the most things. We were placed here to follow The Great Commission. We were chosen to be a people after God's own heart, and we were chosen to love our neighbors as ourselves. To love everyone, even those who upset us, mistreat us, or spitefully use us. We need to stop worrying about all of the things that we don't have, and focus on the 1 thing that we do have, that actually matters, Jesus. Because in the end, nothing that you own comes with you, but Jesus, Jesus will always remain. So don't focus on all of the things you wish you had, focus on the One who means more than all of those things combined. Don't focus on the temporary pleasures of this life, focus on the One that lasts even past this life. Focus, on Jesus.

<u>1 Timothy 6:9-10</u>

What are you chasing in life? Is it money? Here we see that money is the root of all kinds of evil. Some people get so consumed with having more, that they stray from their faith. They have become so focused on having more money, that they have lost their focus on the One thing that matters, God. You see, the enemy wants you consumed with always wanting more, because the longer you take your focus off of God, the more ground he gains in your mind. Let me say this again, the more you allow yourself to focus on the things of this world, the more the enemy gains ground in your mind. Why? Because you have now given the enemy a foothold. You have allowed him to enter thoughts of greed in your mind, and the more you give into the desires of this world, the more ground he will gain. Remember, where your treasure is, there your heart will be also.

For where your treasure is, there your heart will be also.
Matthew 6:21

<u>1 Timothy 6:11-16</u>

Flee from all of these things. Flee from the lusts of this world, and pursue righteousness instead. Pursue *righteousness, godliness, faith, love, patience, gentleness.* Fight. With every ounce of your being, fight. As I have said before, this life is far from easy, and you need to fight. If you come to a fight with no armor, and no weapon, you are as good as dead. Armor up, wake in that armor, sleep in that armor, and don't only armor up, but strengthen that armor, through God's word, and through the Holy Spirit who lives right there inside of you. Don't give the enemy a foothold, rather, put him under your feet! He has no claim on you, and God has given you all the power that you need to trample him, all the power right there inside of you. Keep fighting the good fight of faith. Know that you are not alone, and your brothers and sisters are across the world, fighting alongside you. We may not all know each other, but we are all fighting next to you, in spirit and in heart. Keep pushing forward, share the good news of our Lord and Savior Jesus Christ. If we suffer for this, let it be so. We fight not for the pleasure of man, but we fight for God. We are His warriors. We are God's people. We are His children. Fight for your Father, fight for your Savior who died for you, and fight with the strength of God in you, fight with the Holy Spirit who lives inside of you. The Holy Spirit who is literally God in you. YOU DO NOT FIGHT ALONE! So press on, knowing that one day, one glorious day, in God's timing, we will see our beautiful Savior and Lord Jesus Christ, face to face. The day when we see Him returning in the clouds, the day when He comes to take us home, will be the day that we won't have to fight in this life anymore, we will be where we were always meant to be. With a loving Savior who loves us more than we will ever know. That day, is worth fighting for.

1 Timothy 6:17-20

I would love to end at the last note, because what I wrote felt so powerful in my spirit, but we still have a bit more to go.

Those who are rich, should not be prideful. Remember that whatever you have, was given to you by God. Everything that you own or possess, was approved by God first.

Every good gift and every perfect gift is from above, and comes down from the Father of lights, with whom there is no variation or shadow of turning.

James 1:17

Don't trust in your money, trust in God, who always provides. Money can't speak, but God can. Do good with what you have. Don't hoard your possessions or your money, but share. Being rich in good works is better than being rich in money. Store up good works, rather than a crumbling foundation. Because the time will come, when you face Jesus, and give an account.

Guard what the Lord has given you. Don't buy into false knowledge, and people who try to turn you from your faith.

Be strong in the Lord, and use your armor, with the

help of the Holy Spirit, to guard what you have been entrusted with.

Grace and peace be with you. Amen.

To see more books by Tentmaker Ministries, please go to
Tm-ministries.com